RAILWAYS OF THE WESTERN REGION
IN THE 1970S AND 1980S

Kevin Redwood

AMBERLEY

First published 2019

Amberley Publishing
The Hill, Stroud
Gloucestershire, GL5 4EP

www.amberley-books.com

Copyright © Kevin Redwood, 2019

The right of Kevin Redwood to be identified
as the Author of this work has been asserted in
accordance with the Copyrights, Designs and
Patents Act 1988.

ISBN 978 1 4456 8431 4 (print)
ISBN 978 1 4456 8432 1 (ebook)

British Library Cataloguing in Publication Data.
A catalogue record for this book is available from
the British Library.

Origination by Amberley Publishing.
Printed in the UK.

Introduction

The railways of Britain have been continually evolving, and this was certainly true of the Western Region in the 1970s and 1980s. The photographs in this book were taken between 1977 and 1986 and depict a selection of everyday scenes that show some of the changes taking place.

The introduction of High-Speed Trains (HSTs) in 1976 saw a complete change to the InterCity passenger services across the Western Region. Initially HSTs were introduced on Paddington to Bristol and South Wales services, with specially constructed depots at Old Oak Common and Bristol St Philip's Marsh. The HSTs displaced many of the Class 47s and Class 50s, which in turn allowed the withdrawal of the last Class 52 'Western' hydraulics by February 1977. By May 1980 HST sets were also working into the West of England, where Laira Depot had been upgraded to undertake HST maintenance. From late 1981 HST sets were also introduced onto the North East–South West cross-country route. Across the region, some passenger trains continued to be worked by locos and coaches, including some commuter services out of Paddington and the Portsmouth to Cardiff route, as well as local services in the West Country and West Wales. At Laira, the allocation of Class 25s used on local freight and passenger trains were replaced by an allocation of Class 37s, while the allocation of Class 46 locos were either transferred away to Gateshead or withdrawn.

On the freight network, major changes were taking place. The introduction of the Total Operations Processing System (TOPS) had commenced in 1973, starting in the West Country. TOPS enabled much greater control of the wagon fleet and this, combined with falling freight traffic levels, meant that large numbers of older vacuum-braked or unfitted freight rolling stock could be withdrawn. As most of the remaining traditional goods yards and coal yards also closed, the old vacuum-braked wagonload freight network of services was gradually run down, and finally ceased altogether in 1984. In its place came the Speedlink network, which offered rapid overnight transits across the system. The service conveyed new air-braked wagons, many privately owned, and connected both BR and privately owned freight terminals. Severn Tunnel Junction Yard was an important location, with many Speedlink trunk services from all regions of BR calling night and day.

There were changes too on the signalling side, with semaphore signals being replaced by multiple-aspect colour light signalling, while two new panel signal boxes opened at Westbury and Exeter St David's. The new panel signal box at Westbury opened in May 1984, when stage one of the scheme saw four mechanical signal boxes in the Westbury area closed; by February 1985, the area of control of the new box extended to Somerton.

The new Exeter panel opened in March 1985 when new signals were brought into use in the Exeter St David's station area. Over the months the panel gradually took over a greater area until by October 1987 it controlled the area from Taunton to Totnes.

The Western Region Headquarters were at Paddington and the region was divided into three divisions for operational purposes: the London Division, with headquarters at Reading; the West of England Division, with headquarters at Bristol; and the South Wales Division, with headquarters at Cardiff. Each of the three divisions was different in character. In 1986 the WR HQ moved from Paddington to Swindon, and the three divisional offices were closed.

Paddington station was the most important location on the London Division, with InterCity services running to Bristol, South Wales and the West Country, as well as via the Cotswolds to Gloucester, Cheltenham and Hereford. There were also commuter services to Didcot, Oxford and Newbury, as well as a number of branches. Cross-country services from the North to the South Coast also called at Reading. As well as domestic freight traffic, there was also a lot of inter-regional freight passing through the division. The main marshalling yard was at Acton. The yard declined with the end of the vacuum-braked freight network, but found new use as a staging point for stone traffic from the Mendips. Old Oak Common was the main loco depot, and smaller depots were at Reading, which had an allocation of Class 08s, and Oxford. The DMU fleet was based at Reading, but sets were also outbased at other locations, including Old Oak Common, Southall and Oxford.

Geographically, the West of England Division was the largest, extending from Penzance to just north of Bromsgrove, and there was a contrast between the busy network of lines around Bristol and the sleepy Cornish branch lines. InterCity services included those from Paddington as well as the cross-country route from the North East to the South West, which was very busy on summer Saturdays. The Portsmouth to Cardiff route saw a service frequency that was greatly improved in the early 1980s. Bristol was the hub of a number of commuter services mostly worked by DMUs, as were the branches of Devon and Cornwall. Freight traffic included huge tonnages from the Mendip Quarries and Tytherington in South Gloucestershire. There were several important freight terminals around Bristol and at Avonmouth. China clay provided an important source of revenue from a number of locations in Devon and Cornwall, and was sent to destinations around Britain, with a large amount being exported via the docks at Fowey. The main loco depots were at Bristol Bath Road and Plymouth Laira, each with an allocation of main line locos. Smaller depots at Gloucester, Westbury, Newton Abbot, St Blazey and Penzance each had a small allocation of Class 08 shunters. The DMU fleet was based at Bristol and Plymouth. Bristol sets were also outbased at Worcester, Gloucester, Westbury and Weymouth, while some Plymouth sets were outbased at various locations, including Exeter.

Freight traffic was very important on the South Wales Division, with InterCity passenger traffic being confined to the South Wales Main Line to Cardiff, Swansea and Carmarthen. There was a network of DMU services from Cardiff serving the Valleys, as well as in West Wales, being based in Swansea. Freight traffic was principally coal, steel and oil. Coal from numerous collieries and loading points went to major customers at British Steel at Llanwern and Margam, to Aberthaw Power Station, and for export through Swansea Docks, as well as to coal concentration depots for domestic use. There were also many movements of coal between collieries and washeries, and for blending; this meant that in places it was possible to see loaded coal trains pass one another going in opposite directions. Steel traffic travelled to and from a number of British Steel plants, and included iron ore from Port Talbot to Llanwern. The oil refineries at Milford Haven and Llandarcy dispatched many trains each week. The main loco depots were at Cardiff Canton and Swansea Landore, each with a large allocation of Class 08 shunters, Class 37s and Class 47s. Smaller depots at Ebbw Junction and Margam had allocations of Class 08 shunters. The DMU fleet was allocated to Canton, but were also outbased at Treherbert and Rhymney, with a large number being based at Swansea for use in West Wales.

Most of the photographs were taken between 1978 and 1985, when I worked for BR in the Bristol Area Freight Centre as a TOPS clerk. I made most photographic trips on weekdays by train on my own, armed with a Baker Rail Atlas and an OS map. Some visits were made to Civil Engineers' depots with my father, Norman Redwood, who worked for the Regional Civil Engineers as a wagon supervisor. Later on I made a few trips with my friend and BR colleague Roland Carp, who did the driving. I have always been interested in the unglamorous side of the railway, and hopefully this book will convey something of the everyday atmosphere of the Western Region of the time.

Paddington station on Saturday 4 October 1980 and four High-Speed Train sets are seen in the platforms. The InterCity 125 HSTs had been introduced on the Western Region in 1976 and revolutionised the train service from London to South Wales and the West Country. They would become a familiar sight here for over four decades. The power cars are Nos 43005 (253002), 43015 (253007), 43008 (253004) and 43140 (253035).

A number of locos are seen stabled around the turntable at the back of the depot at Old Oak Common on 27 November 1978. All are Western Region-allocated locos, and from the left to the right they are: Nos 47284 of Bath Road, 47103 of Cardiff Canton, 47129 of Landore and 50020 *Revenge* of Laira, while in the foreground is No. 47069, which is another Cardiff Canton loco.

Many of the local passenger services in the London Division of the Western Region were provided by a large fleet of Pressed Steel Class 117 DMUs based at Reading. On 11 April 1983, set L421 is seen at Acton Main Line, working the 10.30 Slough to London Paddington service. The L prefix indicates it is a London Division set and L421 was formed of vehicles Nos 51359, 59511 and 51401.

Although the HSTs had taken over much of the InterCity passenger work, there were still many loco-and-coach workings on the Region. On 11 April 1983, a Down stopping service from London Paddington, formed of steam-heated Mark 1 stock, pauses at the Down relief platform at Acton Main Line. The loco, No. 47124, is one of Cardiff Canton's steam-heating boiler-fitted locos.

Pressed Steel Class 117 DMU L413 is working the 13.21 Didcot to London Paddington service on 11 April 1983, when seen calling at Slough. Set L413 was formed of vehicles Nos 51349, 59501 and 51391, and was one of twenty-four Pressed Steel-built Class 117 sets allocated to the London Division in the early 1980s.

Once the HST fleet had taken over most of the duties from Paddington to South Wales and the West Country, the Western Region Class 50 fleet found a lot of work on cross-country services, including from Paddington to the North West. On 11 April 1983, No. 50039 *Implacable* calls at Reading with the 14.50 Paddington to Liverpool Lime Street service. No. 50039 had been refurbished and received large logo livery in 1981, and the whole of the Class 50 fleet had been refurbished by the end of 1983.

In the 1950s the Western Region acquired five Ruston & Hornsby 165DE shunting locos for use by the Civil Engineers' department. Much of their work was in the pre-assembly depots (PAD) where new track sections were assembled. No. PWM 653 was new in 1959 and worked at Theale PAD until the depot closed in 1972. Thereafter it was based at Reading and was often found in the Reading Permanent Way Depot, as seen here on 28 November 1978.

The 17.40 Oxford to Paddington local service rounds the curve into Didcot on 8 July 1985, comprising Cardiff-based Class 101 set C812 (formed of vehicles Nos 51462, 59561 and 51533) and Reading-based Class 117 set L420 (formed of vehicles Nos 51358, 59510 and 51400). On the left of the view is Didcot Tip Sidings, where an engineers' train loaded with spent ballast can be seen. In Didcot Yard on the right is another rake of engineers' wagons loaded with spent ballast, and a large number of mineral wagons also now in the engineers' fleet.

On 8 July 1985, No. 50039 *Implacable* departs from Didcot station and crosses Didcot West Junction on a service for the Oxford direction. Behind in the yard can be seen No. 31165 with the 3B07 Paddington to Swansea parcels service. In just three weeks the station would be rebranded as Didcot Parkway.

Coal for Didcot Power Station was an important traffic for BR and it came from a variety of sources, including Yorkshire, the East Midlands and the West Midlands. Class 47 locos had been originally employed on the trains, but from 1976 new Class 56 locos took over most services. Then, in 1983, Class 58 locos started to appear, and seen here rounding the Foxhall Curve with a loaded train from the north on 8 July 1985 is No. 58014. The loco is in the new Railfreight grey livery, and by this date was just over a year old.

One of the important customers for the Speedlink freight network was the Ministry of Defence, who used it to connect depots across the country. Because many of these depots were unable to handle the larger modern air-braked vehicles, 550 vanwides were rebuilt with air brakes and modified suspension, being reclassified as TOPS code VEA for use on MOD traffic. A number of VEAs can be seen behind No. 47217, which is working a service from Didcot to Bicester MOD when seen at Oxford South on 8 July 1985.

A London-bound HST departs Oxford for Paddington on 8 July 1985. In the sidings at Oxford South is Class 117 Pressed Steel DMU set B429, which is formed of vehicles Nos 51367, 59519 and 51409. The B prefix indicates set B429 is allocated to Bristol.

Returning from Bicester MOD Central Ordnance Depot to Didcot is No. 47217, seen passing through Oxford on 8 July 1985. The vehicles include van types VDA, VEA and a single larger VGA.

Problems at Oxford on the morning of 10 July 1981. The 10.21 departure for Paddington, hauled by No. 50002 *Superb*, had been delayed with a defective coach. Assistance had been summoned in the form of Old Oak Common-allocated No. 31259, which has just detached the defective Mark 2 TSO for attention.

By the summer of 1977, the last of the Western Region diesel-hydraulic 'Western' Class 52 locos had been withdrawn from traffic and Swindon Works was engaged in scrapping some of the units. D1005 *Western Venturer* had been built at Swindon in 1962 and was withdrawn from service in November 1976. Here in the yard at Swindon on 9 June 1977, the sad remains of D1005 are being reduced to scrap.

In 1977 Swindon Works was engaged in cutting up foreign locos from other regions including a number of Class 24s. In December 1975 No. 24089 received collision damage in an incident at Bidston Dock. The loco was initially stored as unserviceable, and was then withdrawn from traffic, being moved to Swindon Works in December 1976. When seen at Swindon on 9 June 1977, No. 24089 did not have long to go, being cut up by the end of July 1977.

A Paddington-bound HST headed by power car No. 43133 speeds past Witham Signal Box on 21 June 1984. The signal box here controlled East Somerset Junction and the branch to Foster Yeoman's Merehead Quarry, as well as a bitumen terminal at Cranmore. The signal box closed in November 1984, when control passed to Westbury Panel Signal Box.

Approaching Clink Road Junction on 21 June 1984 is one of the Western Region's named Class 47s. Bath Road-allocated No. 47090 *Vulcan* is working a train of presflos from the Blue Circle Cement Westbury Works to Exeter Central.

Resting in the loco stabling sidings beside Westbury station on 28 February 1979 is No. 31258, one of the Bath Road-allocated Class 31s. For several consecutive years this loco was fitted with miniature snow ploughs for the winter season. Although they were not powerful enough to work the heavier stone trains from the Mendip Quarries, Class 31s found work on engineering trains in the Westbury area, as well as on some of the Bristol to Weymouth passenger services.

Stone traffic from the Mendip Quarries at Merehead and Whatley provided much work for Westbury Depot, and in the early 1980s Class 47s were the preferred motive power for most trains. On Saturday 26 April 1980, with the week's work over, a large number of Class 47s are stabled at Westbury. From left to right they are: Nos 47100, 47027, 47080 *Titan,* 47055, 47240, 47225 and 47063. These were all Western Region locos, except for No. 47100, which was from Crewe Diesel Depot.

Eastleigh-allocated push-pull Class 33/1 locos were not commonly seen on the Western Region in the early 1980s. At Westbury on 21 June 1984, No. 33110 has failed on arrival with the 16.10 Bristol Temple Meads to Portsmouth Harbour service and is about to be assisted forward by No. 47147.

Although Westbury South had already been resignalled with multiple-aspect colour light signals, semaphore signals still remained at Westbury North. Seen from the overbridge at the north end of Westbury station on 14 September 1982, No. 50045 *Achilles* has arrived from Salisbury with Southern Region engineers ballast empties and is in the process of running round the train before continuing westwards to Meldon Quarry. In the station the rear of a train of empty Foster Yeoman PGA hoppers can be seen on their way back to Merehead Quarry.

The Westbury station area was resignalled and the track layout remodelled in April and May 1984; the new layout can be seen here on 21 June 1984. In the platform Bristol-allocated Pressed Steel Class 117 set B435 (formed of vehicles Nos 51373, 59486 and 51415) is leading another set on the 16.25 Weymouth to Bristol Temple Meads. Alongside on the right is No. 47312 from Immingham Depot, which is working 6V83 Speedlink service from Eastleigh to Severn Tunnel Junction.

Prior to the full resignalling of Westbury station in 1984, the signal box at Westbury North had controlled the whole station area. There were semaphore signals at the north end of the station as well as the multiple-aspect signals at the south of the station. On 3 January 1981, No. 47478 waits to depart from Westbury on a service for Paddington.

Just north of Westbury is Hawkeridge Junction. On 16 June 1986, Hither Green-allocated No. 33045 approaches with the 15.10 Bristol Temple Meads to Portsmouth Harbour service. The two lines to the right of the picture curve around to Heywood Road Junction and form part of a useful diversionary route for trains from the Bristol direction that are diverted towards London via the Berks & Hants route.

At Trowbridge on 20 August 1983, the secondman enjoys the summer sunshine as No. 33026 awaits departure with the 15.10 Bristol Temple Meads to Portsmouth Harbour service. Eastleigh-based Class 33s had taken over the working of this route from Bath Road-allocated Class 31/4s in 1980 and in due course the train service increased to be basically hourly between Cardiff/Bristol and Portsmouth Harbour.

In addition to the Bristol to Portsmouth Harbour workings, stations between Bristol and Westbury were also served by Weymouth trains and a number of peak-hours services were worked by DMUs. On 20 August 1983, a pair of DMUs make a smoky departure from Bradford-on-Avon with the 17.11 Bristol Temple Meads to Warminster service. Cardiff-based Metro-Cammell Class 101 set C823 (formed of vehicles Nos 51505, 59082 and 51511) leads Bristol-based Pressed Steel Class 117 set B430 (formed of vehicles Nos 51368, 59520 and 51410).

Between Bristol and Trowbridge, the railway and the River Avon are seldom far apart, with the line crossing the river a number of times. On 23 August 1983, Eastleigh-allocated No. 33022 has just departed from Bradford-on-Avon and immediately crosses the river at the west end of the station. The train is the 06.56 Portsmouth Harbour to Bristol Temple Meads service.

Just running into Bath Spa on 16 June 1986 is HST set No. 253003, forming the 18.15 departure for Bristol Temple Meads. The two power cars and the trailing first class (TFO) at the rear of the train are in the newer InterCity Executive livery.

Passing through Bath Spa on 16 June 1986 is No. 47140, which for many years had been allocated to Bristol Bath Road. The train is 6V83, the Eastleigh to Severn Tunnel Junction Speedlink service. Behind the loco is an empty warflat, TOPS coded PFB, followed by a former BR ferry van, a VEA and a number of discharged bitumen tanks. By this date the former ferry van will be in use as a barrier wagon.

The large marshalling yards at Bristol East Depot closed to revenue-earning traffic in 1967, but both remained in use, with the upside yard becoming a catchment yard for crippled vehicles awaiting repair or assessment while the downside yard became an important civil engineers' depot. On 17 July 1977, No. 31159 departs East Depot Downside with a train of recovered track sections for Taunton Fairwater PAD. Behind the loco is a brake tender; these were still sometimes used on trains of track sections to provide brake force as the engineers' fleet of bogie wagons was largely unfitted.

Kingsland Road Yard in Bristol was a full loads depot, loading and unloading various traffic. Following the closure of the local marshalling yards at Bristol East Depot and Bristol West Depot it also became responsible for the sorting and marshalling of freight traffic for the Bristol area. On 20 September 1983, the yard pilot, No. 08950, is seen at work in the outside part of the yard, which was double-ended, the sidings to the left of the picture being the full loads sidings.

On 20 September 1983, and having just departed Bristol Temple Meads, No. 50007 *Hercules* is seen passing beneath Bristol East Gantry with the 07.40 Penzance to Liverpool Lime Street service. The brick structure on the right is a relay room. It was formerly attached to Bristol East Power Signal Box, which had been demolished after closure in 1970.

Significant snowfall is not common in the Bristol area, but on 11 December 1981 there was a wintry scene at Bristol Temple Meads. On Platform 3, No. 47456 waits with a Plymouth to Manchester Piccadilly service, while on the Up through line is Cardiff-based, Gloucester-built Class 119 set C593 (formed of vehicles Nos 51072, 59431 and 51085).

When Royal Portbury Dock opened in 1978, the import and export of motor vehicles became an important trade. The dock was not to be rail-connected until 2001, but in 1983 BR did gain some traffic, which was road-hauled from Portbury to be loaded to rail in Bristol. On 3 August 1983, No. 47032 is working a local freight trip comprising empty cartic car carriers from Stoke Gifford to Pylle Hill Yard, where they will be loaded with imported cars for conveyance to Leith later that day.

In 1979 the High Level Sidings behind Bristol Temple Meads station were lifted and three new sidings were re-laid, with the intention of being used to stable HST sets then being introduced onto cross-country services. An engineer's train, including recovered scrap track sections, is about to leave the High Level Sidings for Bristol East Depot on 17 July 1979 behind No. 31422. In the event the extra HST sets were always stabled at St Philip's Marsh, and these sidings were used to stable parcel vans.

The Bristol-based DMU fleet was normally fuelled and examined at Marsh Junction. On 18 June 1980, the fuelling point at Marsh Junction is occupied by a Swindon-built Class 120 cross-country DMU. Set C555 (formed of vehicles Nos 51576, 59582 and 51590) is a visitor from Cardiff. In 1983, however, fuelling work was transferred to Bath Road, where the Daily Shed was extended to enable DMUs to be accommodated.

In 1980 Bath Road had an allocation of two Class 03 shunting locos, Nos 03121 and 03382, which were kept specifically for pilot duty at Lawrence Hill Yard. This involved shunting at Avonside Wharf, where the larger Class 08 shunters were not permitted at the time. At Lawrence Hill Yard, No. 03382 is seen on 6 May 1980 attached to the regular runner, No. TDB 709457, which is a former Conflat A. By the following year Class 08 shunters were permitted to work to Avonside Wharf; as a result No. 03121 was withdrawn from service while No. 03382 was transferred to Landore Depot.

The Avonside Wharf branch was part of the remains of the Midland Railway network in Bristol. By the 1970s access to Avonside was via the former GWR yard at Lawrence Hill. The only remaining freight traffic was cement to the Blue Circle cement depot, and seasonal trains of molasses for the distiller's depot. On 28 September 1983, No. 08949 is seen in a scene of urban desolation at Avonside. The train of eighteen tanks of molasses had come from King's Lynn and had been propelled down the branch with the shunters riding in the brake van seen on the middle siding. The tanks would then be berthed in distiller's siding No. 9 at a time.

Bristol Parkway station, which opened in 1972, was the first of the new park and ride stations. Landore-allocated No. 47557 is seen arriving at the Up platform on 18 September 1982. The loco was one of a batch recently converted to Class 47/4 with electric train heating (ETH) equipment and had been renumbered from 47024 in 1979.

One of Cardiff Canton's named Class 47s, No. 47088 *Samson*, is seen at Stoke Gifford Upside on 7 September 1983. It is shunting to form up a train for the ARC quarry at Tytherington. Standing on the Up reception line on the left is a set of ten empty Southern Region seacow hoppers from Woking, which will be loaded with ballast at Tytherington. No. 47088 is about to attach some defective empty PGA hoppers from the Up siding, which are also going to Tytherington, but for repair.

At Avonmouth there were a number of important freight customers, including Commonwealth Smelting, which received large tonnages of coke, and the Port of Bristol Authority (PBA)'s Avonmouth Docks. On 5 February 1981, one of the Bristol area local freight trip locos, No. 31210 of Bath Road, has drawn eight empty HTV hoppers out of the Commonwealth Smelting sidings and past Hallen Marsh Signal Box. The train will reverse and make the short trip up the line to Holesmouth Junction and into the PBA for the hoppers to be loaded with imported house coal at Avonmouth Docks.

Seen shunting at Hallen Marsh on 5 October 1983 is No. 47246. The loco is working local trip No. 78, which served various freight customers in the Avonmouth area. This duty included shunting the rail-served Rowntree's warehouse adjacent to Avonmouth station and was consequently known to many local railwaymen as the 'chocolate' engine. The method of working was for the train to be hauled to Avonmouth, and then after shunting the Rowntree's warehouse it would propel back to Hallen Marsh with the brake van leading. The propelling movement was not permitted during the hours of darkness, or in fog or falling snow.

Commonwealth Smelting at Hallen Marsh received a trainload of coke from South Wales each weekday, while also dispatching lead ingots and tanks of sulphuric acid. As well as a large internal rail network, they also owned their own shunting locos, which were permitted to run out onto BR metals at Hallen Marsh. On 5 October 1983, No. 6, a four-wheel diesel-hydraulic Sentinel shunting loco, hauls wagons into the Smelting Works. The VTG ferrywagon will be used to load lead ingots for export, while the VDA will be for loading to Bloxwich.

A view looking north from Hallen Marsh Signal Box on 5 October 1983. The single line curving away to the left is the Severn Beach line, while heading off to the right is the route to Stoke Gifford. The loco is No. 47246, which is working local trip No. 78 with VDAs for Rowntree's at Avonmouth.

Standing at the end of the line at Severn Beach on 11 February 1980 is single power car Class 121 No. 55033. As set B133, it is working the local service between Bristol Temple Meads and Severn Beach. Although the line now terminated at Severn Beach, until November 1964 there had been a local passenger service through to Pilning (Low Level), but it was a victim of the Beeching cuts.

As well as internal Western Region services, Gloucester also handled inter-regional services from the Midlands and the North. Consequently, locos from a wide area could regularly be seen there. On 6 November 1980, as well as Western Region-based locos, there are two visitors from the London Midland Region. Inside the roofless remains of Horton Road shed are No. 25197 of Manchester Longsight, No. 47026 of Plymouth Laira, an unidentified Peak, No. 31154 of Bristol Bath Road and No. 47050 from Crewe Diesel Depot.

On 4 September 1984, Toton-allocated No. 45108 departs from Platform 4 at Gloucester with the 13.35 service from Cardiff Central to Leeds and Hull. Platform 4 had only just been brought back into passenger use earlier that year, having previously been used as a parcels platform since the 1960s. A new passenger footbridge had also been provided.

Many of the local passenger services in the Gloucester area towards Bristol, Cardiff, Worcester and Swindon were operated by Bristol-based DMUs. Here, Gloucester-built, cross-country Class 119 set B596 (formed of vehicles Nos 51076, 59416 and 51099) waits to depart Gloucester on the 16.40 service to Melksham on 10 July 1985. The station at Melksham had reopened shortly before, on 13 May 1985, under the terms of the Speller Act, having previously been closed by BR in 1966.

Following the closure of the former Midland station at Gloucester Eastgate in 1975, all services called at the GWR Gloucester Central station. This, however, meant that some trains had to reverse before continuing their journey, which added interest, but could cause operating problems at times. On 10 July 1985, No. 47553 had recently arrived at Gloucester on a Paddington to Cheltenham service and been replaced by a Class 45 for the final leg of the journey. 1E21, the 14.15 Plymouth to Leeds parcels, arrives behind No. 47088. This train will then reverse direction.

London Division DMUs were commonly seen in the Worcester area, often working in on services from Oxford. Here at Worcester Shrub Hill on 12 February 1982, Reading-based, Pressed Steel Class 117 set L419 (formed of vehicles Nos 51356, 59508 and 51398) arrives on a service from Hereford. In the background, No. 25211 can be seen stabled in Worcester Depot.

Newland Sidings were located between Worcester and Great Malvern and in 1954 they became a pre-assembly depot (PAD), making up new track sections for use on relaying sites around the Western Region. Ruston & Hornsby 165DE shunting loco No. PWM 654 came here in 1964 having previously worked at Hookagate Depot near Shrewsbury. Seen at Newland PAD receiving attention on 27 March 1979, loco No. PWM 654 was the regular Newland loco until the depot closed in 1982.

In the summer of 1981, Southern Region Class 33s took over the haulage of passenger services between Cardiff and Crewe, replacing Midland Region Class 25s. Seen at Hereford is Eastleigh-allocated No. 33014, which is working the 11.50 Cardiff Central to Crewe service on 12 February 1982.

The North & West Route via Hereford handled a lot of freight, much of it through traffic from Scotland and the North West to South Wales and the West Country, but some of it coming from intermediate locations along the route. Earlier, No. 47285 had arrived at Hereford on 12 February 1982 with a solitary vanwide from the Royal Army Ordnance Corps depot at Moreton-on-Lugg. The Hereford yard pilot loco had then attached traffic, including a discharged tank and five empty BDAs, which had delivered steel to the Painter Brothers works at Hereford. The train will shortly depart southwards for Severn Tunnel Junction.

By 1986 it was becoming increasingly rare to see Peaks working west of Bristol, as all the remaining Class 45s were allocated to Toton. Meldon Quarry ballast services still provided some work for the class. Here, on 6 November 1986, No. 45062 is seen passing the site of Flax Bourton station with 6B54, the Bristol East Depot to Meldon train, which is formed of five empty sealion and seacow ballast hoppers.

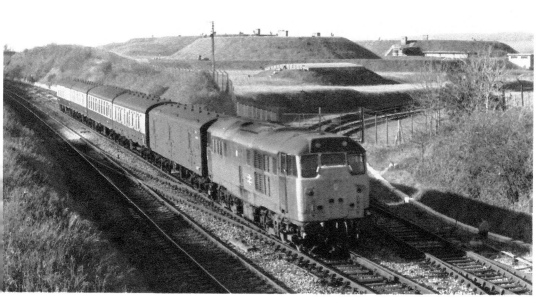

Most local passenger services between Bristol and Weston-super-Mare were worked by DMUs, but most years there were one or two trains diagrammed for loco and coaches. An unusual set of Mark 1 stock forms the consist for Old Oak Common's No. 31465 as it passes Flax Bourton with the 11.50 Weston-super-Mare to Bristol Temple Meads service on 6 November 1986. In the background is the Flax Bourton Petroleum Supply Depot, which was part of the Government Pipelines & Storage System; although rail-connected, the sidings were disused.

Yatton had been a junction for branches to Clevedon and the Cheddar Valley, but although both had closed in the 1960s, the station had become important for commuters to Bristol and retained a good local train service. On Saturday 25 June 1983, No. 50012 *Benbow* speeds through the Down platform, heading west. The former Clevedon bay platform can be seen on the left.

On a bitterly cold afternoon, the frost is still on the sleepers at Weston-super-Mare despite the low winter sun. The 10.30 Sundays-only Liverpool Lime Street to Plymouth service runs into the station on 13 January 1980; the passengers will be glad of the steam heating provided by No. 47030.

January 1982 was one of the rare occasions when significant snow fell in Weston-super-Mare and did not melt straight away. On 11 January 1982, two trains for Bristol are in the platforms. One of them, Bristol-based Class 121 No. 55032, set B132, stands under the footbridge. It was rare to see one in Weston, but a special timetable was in operation that day. Meanwhile, No. 31118, one of Bath Road's boiler-fitted Class 31s, stands in the Up platform, awaiting departure.

Both platforms at Weston-super-Mare are signalled for reversible working, but where possible most trains will call at Platform 2, which is the main platform. On 11 January 1982, No. 47171 departs from Platform 2 with a service for Taunton formed of steam-heated Mark 1 stock.

The proposal for the Bristol & Exeter Railway main line to pass close to the centre of Weston-super-Mare was opposed by local landowners. As a result, it was not until 1884 that the present station opened after the GWR constructed the Weston loop line. At Uphill Junction, No. 50016 *Barham* comes off the loop line with the 06.35 service from Bristol Temple Meads to Plymouth on 15 June 1982. This train was one of a number of services in the West Country diagrammed to be formed of a short set of Mark 1 coaches, and also conveyed booked parcel vans for Plymouth.

Bleadon & Uphill station closed in October 1964. For some years the station then became the site of the small Yieldingtree Railway Museum, with exhibits including former GWR 0-4-0ST No. 1338 and a Hunslet 0-4-0T. On 15 June 1982, the museum had been closed for some time, but some exhibits remained. Cardiff-based, Swindon-built cross-country Class 120 set C616 (formed of vehicles Nos 51782, 59681 and 51790) passes the site of the station, working the 08.40 Taunton to Bristol Temple Meads.

Once the Southern Region Class 33s had taken over the Portsmouth Harbour to Cardiff services, the diagrams also included local services from Bristol to Weston-super-Mare and Taunton. At Highbridge on Saturday 28 July 1984, the 18.15 departure for Taunton is worked by No. 33030.

At Bridgwater on 12 September 1980, Bescot-allocated No. 47335 prepares to restart 7M22, the 09.05 Exeter Riverside to Bescot service. The train was booked to call at Bridgwater to attach a flatrol with a loaded nuclear flask from the Hinkley Point Nuclear Power Station, which was then conveyed on normal wagonload services to Sellafield.

For several years Bridgwater yard was shunted by a Class 08, which worked up from Taunton each weekday. Just arriving at Bridgwater on 12 September 1980 is No. 08281 with 8B05, the 06.55 trip from Taunton to Bridgwater. Behind the brake van is a discharged nuclear flask from Sellafield. As well as shunting at Bridgwater, the loco would also make a local trip up the line to Huntspill with traffic for the Royal Ordnance Factory at Puriton.

From 1981 nuclear flask traffic to and from Sellafield no longer passed on ordinary wagonload trains, but was moved on special dedicated services. On 9 August 1983, No. 47202 is seen soon after arrival at Bridgwater with 7V52, the flask train from Sellafield. The wagons are being shunted into the crane compound.

Bridgwater station was opened by the Bristol & Exeter Railway in 1841, and the Brunel-designed building is now Grade II listed. On 9 August 1983, a local service from Taunton to Bristol Temple Meads calls, formed by Bristol-based BRCW Class 118 set B472 (comprising vehicles Nos 51315, 59482 and 51330).

A summer Saturday service for the West Country approaches Taunton East on 1 September 1984. The view, taken from the new O'Bridge over the railway, sees No. 45029 on the Down relief being signalled into the Down platform. The adjacent signal shows that another train is due on the Down main.

A number of locos and items of stock were repainted to commemorate 150 years of the GWR. Among them was No. 50007 *Hercules,* which was repainted in Brunswick Green and renamed *Sir Edward Elgar* in February 1984. On 1 September 1984, No. 50007 *Sir Edward Elgar* rounds the curve into Taunton with a service for Paignton.

At Taunton on 8 April 1980, No. 47015 departs with the 07.56 Cardiff Central to Plymouth service. It is signalled on the Down relief line, which it will take as far as Silk Mill Crossing, to allow the following 07.30 Paddington to Penzance service to overtake on the Down main line.

Bescot-allocated No. 47479 approaches Taunton with a summer Saturday service for Glasgow Central on 1 September 1984. The train is passing the impressive west gantry, with the popular photographer's vantage point of Forty Steps footbridge in the background.

A view taken from Forty Steps footbridge at Taunton West. On 23 July 1983, a summer Saturday service for Paignton departs Taunton on the Down relief line and passes the west gantry behind No. 50049 *Defiance*.

One of the important gains by BR during the Speedlink era was cider traffic from the Taunton Cider Co. at Norton Fitzwarren. The firm loaded cider from a siding that was actually part of the Minehead branch. On 23 July 1983, Tinsley-allocated No. 45017 passes the siding with a summer Saturday service for the West Country.

Toton-allocated No. 45070 passes the site of Norton Fitzwarren Junction on 23 July 1983 with a summer Saturday service from the West Country. The overgrown West Somerset Railway branch to Minehead curves away on the right, and until 1966 there had also been the Devon & Somerset Railway line to Barnstaple, which branched off between the two lines.

Partway up the notorious Wellington Bank, between Wellington and Whiteball Tunnel, is Beambridge, where the A38 crosses the railway. The steepest part of the gradient here is 1 in 80. On 17 August 1985, No. 47212 heads up the bank with a summer Saturday service for the west.

The gradient up to Whiteball Tunnel from the west is 1 in 115. Approaching the Down loop at Whiteball, No. 47519 is nearing the summit with a Saturday service for Manchester Piccadilly on 25 May 1985.

A CrossCountry HST service for the west approaches Tiverton Junction on 25 May 1985. Tiverton Junction was formerly the junction for branches to Tiverton and Hemyock, and the truncated remains of the Hemyock branch can be seen on the right in this view.

The 07.30 Paddington to St Austell Motorail service speeds through Tiverton Junction behind No. 47061 on Saturday 28 July 1984. By this date few trains called here and the station was a shadow of its former self. The station closed on 11 May 1986, when the new station at Tiverton Parkway opened.

At Crediton, Plymouth-based Class 118 DMU set P462 (formed of vehicles Nos 51304, 59477 and 51319) departs the station, working the 09.00 Exeter St David's to Barnstaple on 31 October 1983. The signalman is seen returning to his box after handing over the single line token to the driver. From here to the site of the former Coleford Junction, the two single lines to Meldon Quarry and Barnstaple run parallel to one another.

Although a couple of passenger trains each day on the Barnstaple branch were worked by a loco and coaches, the majority of services were worked by DMUs. Another Plymouth-based Class 118 DMU, set P463 (formed of vehicles Nos 51305, 59472 and 51320), stands at Barnstaple on 31 October 1983.

The hard hornfels rock found at Meldon was ideal for use as track ballast and the London & South Western Railway opened a quarry here in 1874. Over the years the quarry was expanded to supply ballast to the whole Southern Railway network, and by the 1970s the Western Region also received significant amounts. For many years the quarry had a series of resident steam locos for shunting purposes; in later years, the Class 08 diesel shunter was supplied by Newton Abbot Depot, and on 9 July 1981, No. 08668 can be seen at work in the sidings.

On 31 October 1983 there is a busy scene at Exeter St David's. On the left, No. 50046 *Ajax* awaits departure from Platform 5 with a Plymouth to Glasgow and Edinburgh service; meanwhile, No. 47381 approaches Red Cow Crossing with 6B39, the Severn Tunnel Junction to St Blazey Speedlink service. On the right, No. 50023 *Howe* heads towards the loco spur after arriving on the 06.32 service from Salisbury.

There were a number of freight terminals in Exeter that were served by local freight trip workings. At Exeter St David's on 9 July 1985 is Toton-allocated No. 45012, working from the Blue Circle cement depot at Exeter Central to Exeter Riverside Yard. The empty PCAs are for Westbury Cement Works.

The resignalling of the Exeter St David's station area took place in April and May 1985, and this included removal of the Down through line. The revised layout is seen here on 9 July 1985. On the left, No. 50017 *Royal Oak* has just arrived on the 06.29 service from Salisbury, while No. 31260 shunts to attach an empty newspaper GUV to the empty news van train to Old Oak Common.

On Saturday 28 July 1984, the 10.10 service from Barnstaple has just arrived at Exeter St David's behind Bath Road-allocated No. 31230. Bath Road Class 31s had been regularly seen in the Exeter area since the mid-1970s, and took over more work from 1980 once the Laira allocation of Class 25s was transferred away.

One of the numerous Class 50 locos allocated to Laira, No. 50021 *Rodney*, makes a smoky departure as it heads west from Exeter St David's on 16 July 1980. It would be another sixteen months before it was called to Doncaster Works as part of the Class 50 refurbishment programme.

By 1984 all fifty Class 50s had been refurbished. Laira-allocated No. 50048 *Dauntless*, in large logo livery, heads west from Exeter St David's with ballast-loaded seacows on 11 July 1984.

All routes received an annual visit by a weedspray train, one of which was operated by Chipman's, which is seen here in the yard at Exeter St David's on 21 April 1982. The weedspray train, worked by No. 33004, is standing on the former Up freight avoiding line. On the adjacent line stands No. 50001 *Dreadnought* with a set of stock arrived off a service from Waterloo.

After the Exeter area resignalling had taken place in 1985, there was a revised track layout in the stabling point at Exeter St David's. On 9 July 1985, a number of locos are stabled in and around the remains of the former steam shed.

The steep gradient up from Exeter St David's to Exeter Central has always caused problems; in steam days, up to three additional assisting engines were sometimes required. On 15 May 1979, No. 25223, seen working a local trip from Exeter Riverside to Exmouth Junction, is assisted out of Exeter St David's by No. 25057. Both locos were allocated to Laira Depot.

In July 1984, work on the Exeter Area resignalling scheme was well advanced, with new colour light signals having been installed but not yet in use. A Paignton to Paddington service arrives at Exeter St David's on 28 July 1984 behind No. 47575. In the left background is Exeter West Signal Box, which closed in May 1985.

Immingham-allocated No. 31158, in large logo Railfreight livery, descends down the bank from Exeter Central into Exeter St David's on 9 July 1985 with inspection saloon No. 999508.

Southern Region Class 33s took over the operation of the Waterloo to Exeter route in October 1971, replacing the Warship diesel-hydraulics that had taken over from steam haulage in 1964. On 15 May 1979, No. 33019 calls at Exeter Central with the 12.28 Exeter St David's to Waterloo service.

The 11.10 Waterloo to Exeter St David's approaches Exeter Central behind Eastleigh-allocated No. 33008 *Eastleigh* on 11 March 1983. By this date it was unusual to see a Class 33 in passenger service on the route as WR Class 50s had been diagrammed to the services since May 1980.

On the first Down service of the day on 11 March 1983, No. 50003 *Temeraire* arrives at Exeter Central with the 06.32 Salisbury to Exeter St David's. The Class 50s had been cascaded to this route following the introduction of HSTs on domestic services out of Paddington.

Two of the Plymouth-based, BRCW Class 118 DMU sets meet at Exeter Central on 17 July 1985. On the left, set P465 (formed of vehicles Nos 51307, 59474 and 51322) is working from Exmouth to Exeter St David's, while on the right, set P468 (formed of vehicles Nos 51310, 59471 and 51325) is heading to Exmouth.

Although it escaped closure from the Beeching Report, the Exmouth branch was rationalised in 1973 to just a single line, with one passing loop at Topsham, where two Class 118 BRCW DMUs are seen on 11 March 1983. Set P464 (formed of vehicles Nos 51306, 59473 and 51321) is working the 16.14 Exmouth to Exeter Central when seen, while set P461 (formed of vehicles Nos 51303, 59470 and 51318) is working the 16.11 Exeter St David's to Exmouth.

The branch to Exmouth is the busiest of the branch lines in Devon and Cornwall, and Exmouth station once boasted four platforms. The new station at Exmouth opened in May 1976 and the single platform shared facilities with the adjacent bus station. Class 118 set P461 has just arrived from Exeter and will shortly return as the 14.25 departure for Exeter St David's on 9 July 1985.

Class 50s were first transferred to the Western Region in the early 1970s and soon became a familiar sight. On summer Saturdays they worked many inter-regional cross-country trains, as well as services from Paddington. At 14.48 on Saturday 11 August 1984, No. 50019 *Ramillies* was one of seven members of the class to pass through Dawlish Warren within an hour. Here, it heads towards Exeter with a train from the West Country.

The well-known camping coaches have been a feature at Dawlish Warren since they were first introduced by the GWR in the 1930s. An HST service for the west passes through Dawlish Warren on the Down main line on Saturday 30 June 1984.

On Saturday 13 August 1983, Toton-allocated No. 45065 comes to the rescue of a failed HST and is seen heading westwards through Dawlish Warren.

On summer Saturdays the large number of trains to and from the west meant that many locos normally restricted to freight-only work were pressed into passenger service. A train for Newcastle passes along the Dawlish sea wall on 30 June 1984 behind a loco with an isolated train-heating boiler, Tinsley-allocated No. 45010.

Large logo No. 50029 *Renown* is approaching Dawlish with a train for the West Country on Saturday 30 June 1984.

By the 1980s the signal box at Dawlish had been downgraded to a 'summer Saturdays only' box when it was switched in to cope with the additional traffic. On the evening of Saturday 9 July 1983, No. 47512 of Old Oak Common passes the box with a train for the west.

At Dawlish one of Stratford's silver-roofed locos, No. 47155, bursts out of Kennaway Tunnel and meets an unidentified classmate heading west on Saturday 19 July 1980.

Crewe Diesel-allocated No. 47119 is one of the locos with an isolated steam-heating boiler that was normally confined to freight work. It is seen here on the sea wall at Teignmouth with a service for Paignton on Saturday 21 July 1984.

On a fine summer evening, Old Oak Common-allocated No. 47502 rounds the curve into Teignmouth, heading west, on 3 July 1984.

Seen from the Shaldon Bridge with Teignmouth in the background, one of the CrossCountry HST sets heads up the Teign Estuary towards Newton Abbot on 3 July 1982.

Old Oak Common Depot had a number of named ETH-fitted Class 47/4s, including No. 47510 *Fair Rosamund*, which is seen passing Newton Abbot East Signal Box with the 08.57 Paddington to Paignton service on 3 July 1982.

A Penzance-bound service in the charge of No. 50024 *Vanguard* calls at Newton Abbot on Saturday 20 July 1985.

On 5 November 1981 in Newton Abbot there were three ETH-fitted Class 31/4s at work, including Bath Road-allocated No. 31424, which is just departing for Paignton with the 09.35 service from Exeter St David's.

Laira Depot had an allocation of Class 25s for local work from 1971 until 1980, when the last examples were transferred away or withdrawn. One of the locos to survive was No. 25058, seen here at Newton Abbot on 21 July 1980. It was reallocated to Bescot in October that year. The other locos are Tinsley's No. 45063, Laira's No. 46001 and No. 45054 from Toton.

As there were normally no booked DMU workings between Exeter and Taunton, it was unusual to see DMUs from other depots at work in Devon and Cornwall. It was a surprise, therefore, to see Bristol-based Gloucester-built Class 119 set B591, which is seen heading east through Newton Abbot on the Up through line on 20 July 1985.

Departing Newton Abbot for Paignton on 9 July 1983 is No. 45104 *The Royal Warwickshire Fusiliers*. By this date Newton Abbot Depot, seen in the background, had closed.

Summer Saturdays in the west were very busy, with both domestic Western Region and inter-regional services, as seen here on Saturday 3 July 1982. Just departing Newton Abbot is No. 50015 *Valiant* with the 09.30 Paddington to Paignton service. Meanwhile, No. 47240 approaches with the 12.20 Paignton to Manchester Piccadilly.

On Saturday 9 July 1983, in between the frequent passenger trains full of holidaymakers a pair of HST power cars, Nos 43164 and 43188, pass Aller Junction on their way to Laira Depot.

On Saturday 9 July 1983, more than twenty Class 45s were at work in the West. Coming off the Paignton line at Aller Junction is Tinsley-allocated No. 45015.

One of the last Class 50s to be refurbished was No. 50027 *Lion*, seen here in un-refurbished condition on Saturday 31 July 1982. It is making a smoky departure from Paignton with the 16.13 Paignton to Oxford.

At Paignton on Saturday 31 July 1982, a service has just arrived behind an unidentified ETH-fitted Class 47/4. On the right is the Paignton & Dartmouth Steam Railway, with former BR Class 03 shunter D2192, now named *Ardent*, in the siding.

A busy scene at Goodrington carriage sidings on Saturday 31 July 1982, with two Old Oak Common Class 50s stabled ready to work return services away from Paignton later that day. On the left, No. 50027 *Lion* will work back to Oxford, while on the right, standby loco No. 50040 *Leviathan* is attached to failed loco No. 47447 with a train for Swansea.

During the summer season, a number of services ran from Scotland and the north of England, starting on Friday evening and running overnight to the West Country. At 10.20 in the morning of Saturday 3 July 1982, No. 47447 accelerates through Totnes with an overnight service from Edinburgh.

A general view of Laira Depot in Plymouth on 22 September 1980. At the beginning of 1980, Laira had an allocation of ninety-three locos, comprising seven Class 08s, ten Class 25s, two Class 37s, twenty Class 46s, fourteen Class 47s and thirty-nine Class 50s. The locos in this view include Nos 46017, 47138, 25223 and 47475. The Class 46 and the Class 25 were at their home depot.

The 07.40 service from Penzance to Liverpool Lime Street stands at Plymouth on 15 November 1982. The loco, No. 50031 *Hood*, is allocated to Old Oak Common.

Although listed for closure in the Beeching Report, the branch from Bere Alston to Gunnislake had escaped closure as Gunnislake had poor road connections. To work the steeply graded line, Laira had a two-car Class 118 DMU with the centre trailer car removed. On 22 September 1980, set P480 (formed of vehicles Nos 51312 and 51327) is seen reversing at Bere Alston while working the 14.15 service from Gunnislake to Plymouth.

Wenford Bridge was one of a number of china clay loading points in Cornwall, but main-line locos were not permitted to work over the branch from Boscarne Junction. From Monday to Friday each week, a St Blazey-allocated Class 08 shunter would work clay trains between Bodmin Road, Boscarne Junction and Wenford Bridge. After finishing work on 15 April 1983, No. 08113 is seen at Bodmin Road on its return to St Blazey.

Class 37s had replaced Class 25s on local freight work in Cornwall in 1980. One of the replacements, Laira-allocated No. 37274, is seen shunting at Lostwithiel with clayhoods of export clay for Fowey on 23 June 1982. Trains from clay loading points in the St Austell area, such as this one, were required to reverse at Lostwithiel before proceeding down the branch to Fowey.

A Paddington to Penzance service runs into the Down platform at Par, formed by HST set No. 253006, with power car No. 43013 leading on 21 April 1982.

One of Laira's large allocation of Class 50s, No. 50009 *Conqueror*, arrives at Par with 3S15, the 12.15 Paignton to Glasgow Salkeld Street parcels service on 21 April 1982. This was one of the most heavily loaded services in Cornwall, being permitted to load up to 490 tons.

Plymouth-allocated Class 118/116/118 DMU set P469 (formed of vehicles Nos 51311, 59340 and 51326) stands at Newquay on 23 June 1982, waiting to form the 16.20 departure for Par. Three platforms were required to handle the additional long-distance services on summer Saturdays, but on normal weekdays Newquay was poorly served, with only seven trains a day.

Cornish china clay traffic originated from various locations, including a number of places along the branch from Burngullow to Parkandillack. On 8 March 1983, Laira-allocated No. 37274 heads empty clay hoods from Fowey for Drinnick Mill on the branch, and is seen passing through St Austell.

Local passenger services on the Cornish Main Line were often worked by a loco and coaches sometimes with parcel vans attached to the rear. One train was 1B59, the 13.45 Penzance to Bristol Temple Meads, which is seen calling at St Austell on 15 April 1983 behind No. 45137 *The Bedfordshire and Hertfordshire Regiment (TA)*. The sidings to the right serve the St Austell Motorail terminal.

The same train is seen again the following year, this time at Truro. On 8 March 1983, the 13.45 Penzance to Bristol Temple Meads is hauled by No. 45128, which is another Toton-allocated Class 45/1 ETH-fitted loco. This loco was one of the last of the class to have the headcode panels plated over.

At the end of the line at Penzance, HST set No. 253025, with power car No. 43051 leading, waits to form the 15.37 service to Paddington on 16 July 1980. Now displaced from such services, No. 50026 *Indomitable,* on the left, waits with a parcels train.

Severn Tunnel Junction was the railway gateway to South Wales, and many freight trains called at the extensive marshalling yards here. On 9 September 1980, one of the Class 08 yard pilots, No. 08932, has just finished propelling a train over the Down hump. Up to six Class 08s were employed here, initially being supplied from Ebbw Junction, and later from Cardiff Canton Depot.

The 07.50 Cardiff Central to Portsmouth Harbour passes through Severn Tunnel Junction behind Hither Green-allocated No. 33046 on 16 June 1983.

Locos from a large number of different depots worked into Severn Tunnel Junction on freight services from all regions of BR. Stabled inside the shed on 9 September 1980 is Gateshead-allocated No. 46051.

Arriving at Undy Yard at the west end of Severn Tunnel Junction is Landore-allocated No. 37237, which is working 6C36, the Llanwern to Swindon Speedlink service on 25 September 1986. This train principally conveyed steel products, including coil for the BL car body plant at Swindon.

An unidentified HST working the 07.00 Paddington to Swansea service is seen crossing the River Usk on the approach to Newport on 7 May 1985.

On Friday 12 July 1985, a relief service was provided for the 15.00 Paddington to Swansea. It is seen here approaching Newport at 16.50 behind No. 31191, which was an unusual visitor from Immingham.

The through lines at Newport were often busy with passing freight traffic, and on 4 September 1984 one of Cardiff Canton's large allocation of Class 47s, No. 47238, heads west with discharged 100-ton tanks.

The short-distance traffic of steel coil from the British Steel Llanwern Works to Newport Docks was one of very few revenue-earning flows to be still conveyed in unfitted vehicles by 1985. At Gaer Junction, No. 37204 heads back towards Llanwern with empty Coil C and Coil J wagons on 7 May 1985. In the background, a train for British Steel Ebbw Vale disappears into Gaer Tunnel.

The heaviest trains in South Wales were the iron ore trains from Port Talbot Docks to BSC Llanwern, each formed of twenty-seven wagons. Pairs of Class 56s were introduced to the working in August 1979, replacing triple-headed Class 37s. On 25 September 1986, Nos 56048 and 56032 *Sir de Morgannwg/County of South Glamorgan* accelerate past Waterloo Loop Signal Box, near Newport.

Machen Quarry, west of Newport, was an important supplier of track ballast for the Western Region. On 25 September 1986, No. 37181 approaches Park Junction with a loaded train from Machen comprising eleven dogfish hoppers, with two sealion hoppers at the rear.

Ebbw Junction Diesel Depot opened in 1966. Although there had been main-line locos allocated here, by 1982 the allocation comprised nineteen Class 08 shunting locos. One of the Ebbw Junction-based locos, No. 08822, stands outside the depot on 25 January 1982. The loco without buffers seen alongside is No. 37264. The depot had closed by 1985.

Cardiff Canton had a large allocation of DMUs, including over twenty Derby-built Class 116 suburban sets for services in the Cardiff Valleys. Departing Cardiff Central on 21 July 1982 is Class 116 set C319 (formed of vehicles Nos 50868, 59031 and 50918).

Class 25s allocated to Crewe Diesel Depot had been diagrammed to work passenger services over the Cardiff to Crewe route since 1976, and would continue to do so until replaced by Southern Region Class 33s in 1981. On 10 September 1979, No. 25245 is seen at Cardiff Central having arrived on the 12.25 service from Crewe. Set C452 alongside is one of the Cardiff-based DMUs and is formed of mixed Class 117/116/117s; namely, vehicles Nos 51339, 59446 and 51382.

Approaching Cardiff Central from the west on 14 April 1983 is one of Cardiff Canton's large allocation of Class 37s, No. 37270. Part of Canton Depot can be seen in the background. The train includes a number of the distinctive BR Ford palvans.

Accelerating through Barry, an empty MGR train from Aberthaw Power Station is hauled by Nos 37297 and 37205 on 21 July 1982. The coal for the power station came from various collieries in the Cardiff Valleys, as well as in the Swansea area. Around 100 coal trains ran per week, each formed of twenty-eight hoppers and hauled by pairs of Class 37s.

Swinging round the curve into Barry station on 21 July 1982 is the 10.50 service from Barry Island to Merthyr, formed by Cardiff-based Class 116 set C307 (formed of vehicles Nos 50083, 59031 and 50820).

Penarth station had become a terminus in 1968 when the route onwards via Lavernock and Sully closed. On 7 May 1985, Class 116 set C317 (formed of vehicles Nos 53858, 59446 and 53911) waits to head back to Cardiff Central.

At the reception sidings at Aberthaw on 12 November 1985, Nos 37205 and 37240 have just been detached from a loaded MGR train from Ogmore. To take the train around the Aberthaw Power Station loop, one of the slow-speed Canton-based Class 47s will be attached to the rear of the train.

At Deep Navigation Colliery in Treharris on 24 May 1983, No. 37251 waits to depart with a train of colliery shale loaded in 33-ton former iron ore hoppers. The shale will be unloaded at a tip at nearby Nelson Bog.

A loaded MGR train from Deep Navigation Colliery, headed by Class 37s Nos 37255 and 37300, is seen standing at the site of the closed Trelewis Halt before heading for Aberthaw Power Station on 24 May 1983.

The station at Rhymney became a terminus in 1954, when the route northwards to Rhymney Bridge closed. At Rhymney, Cardiff-based Class 116 set C302 (formed of vehicles Nos 50086, 59036 and 50128) waits to head south on the 10.28 service to Penarth on 14 April 1981.

Radyr Yard was the main marshalling point for wagonload freight to and from the Cardiff Valleys. On 26 June 1981, one of Cardiff Canton's large allocation of Class 08 shunters, No. 08898, is seen at Radyr station when making a shunt movement out of the yard.

The majority of passenger services in the Cardiff Valleys were operated by Derby-built, three-car Class 116 suburban DMUs. One of Cardiff Canton's Class 116 sets, C318 (formed of vehicles Nos 50864, 59369 and 50917), departs from Radyr, heading south towards Cardiff on 3 November 1981.

To handle the large tonnage of coal from the numerous collieries in the valleys, there had been four tracks from Radyr to Pontypridd – though by the 1980s colliery closures meant that the relief lines had been taken out of use north of Taffs Well. Swindon-built, Cardiff-based, cross-country Class 120 set C560 (formed of vehicles Nos 51581, 59587 and 51585) approaches Taffs Well with the 08.58 Merthyr to Cardiff Central service on 28 November 1980.

A number of Cardiff Canton-allocated Class 37s were outbased at Radyr to work freight trip workings in the valleys. On 24 May 1983, No. 37239 heads south towards Taffs Well with a fully fitted train of Phurnacite from Abercwmboi to Severn Tunnel Junction.

The Phurnacite plant at Abercwmboi in the Cynon Valley was an important freight customer, receiving large amounts of coal from various collieries for processing, and then forwarding the smokeless fuel Phurnacite to coal depots across the BR network. On 24 May 1983, No. 37239 departs Abercynon with coal for Abercwmboi from Merthyr Vale Colliery.

Standing in the platform at Abercynon is Cardiff-based Class 116 set C313 (formed of vehicles Nos 53847, 59040 and 53900), which is working the 08.42 Cardiff Central to Merthyr on 24 May 1983.

The National Coal Board purchased a number of former BR shunting locos and two Class 08 shunters, D3014 and D3183, went to Merthyr Vale Colliery. One of the pair is seen standing near the weighbridge at the colliery on 14 April 1983.

The 10.52 Cardiff Central to Merthyr service heads past Merthyr Vale Colliery on 14 April 1983, being worked by Cardiff-based Class 116 set C303 (formed of vehicles Nos 50087, 59037 and 50129).

One of Cardiff Canton's Class 101 Metro-Cammell DMU sets approaches Merthyr Vale on 14 April 1983. Set C811 (formed of vehicles Nos 51801, 59548 and 51519) is working the 10.00 Merthyr to Cardiff Central service.

Merthyr was served by a service from Barry Island that ran more or less hourly during the day. On 23 November 1982, Cardiff-based Class 116 DMU set C330 (formed of vehicles Nos 51128, 59357 and 51141) stands in the one remaining platform at Merthyr before returning south.

Although Treherbert station at the head of the Rhondda Valley was once on a through route via the Rhondda & Swansea Bay Railway to Aberavon and Swansea, passenger services ceased in 1968 and the station is now a terminus. On 10 September 1979, Class 116 DMU set C315 (formed of vehicles Nos 50855, 59363 and 50908) waits in refurbished livery to work the 13.15 service to Cardiff Central.

To produce Phurnacite, the plant at Abercwmboi required a mixture of different grades of coal to be blended, and one source was Onllwyn. A fully fitted train of coal from Onllwyn for Abercwmboi passes Pyle, to the west of Bridgend, behind No. 37228 on 12 November 1985.

Among the loading points that supplied coal to Aberthaw Power Station, some were located to the west of Aberthaw, including Blaenant and Jersey Marine, and these were reached via the Vale of Glamorgan route to Bridgend. On 7 July 1981, Nos 37291 and 37231 head west past Port Talbot Panel Signal Box with an empty MGR train from Aberthaw.

A Paddington to Swansea HST service has just departed from Neath station on 9 November 1983. The leading power car is seen crossing the Tennant Canal, while to the right is the River Neath.

Most services from Swansea to lines in West Wales were worked by DMUs, but there were also a number of loco-hauled trains into the 1980s. On 6 June 1983, No. 47536 stands at Swansea, ready to work the 10.17 departure for Fishguard Harbour.

Export coal for Ireland through Swansea Docks continued to be loaded in unfitted 21-ton mineral wagons (TOPS code MDO) until 1987, long after unfitted trains had ceased to run on many parts of the BR network. On 19 September 1986, yard pilot No. 08780 shunts a rake of loaded MDOs out of Swansea Burrows Sidings. This train had just arrived from Onllwyn.

As well as export coal traffic, Swansea Burrows also handled traffic for the Ford car plant, and the wagon repair depot at Port Tennant. On 19 September 1986, Swansea Burrows' yard pilot, No. 08780, shunts in the 'A' set sidings. The Danygraig Freightliner terminal can just be seen in the distance.

Swansea's King's Dock, with yard pilot No. 08367 hauling MDOs of export coal out of the holding sidings and past King's Dock Junction Signal Box on 19 September 1986.

The export coal for Swansea Docks came from a number of collieries and washeries in West Wales. Here, on 4 November 1983, No. 37279 heads west through Llanelli with empty unfitted MDOs.

Class 33s had been working passenger services to Cardiff since 1981, but from May 1982 they also began working some of the West Wales passenger services. On 24 June 1982, Eastleigh-allocated No. 33024 calls at Llanelli on a service for Swansea.

By 1983 the traditional vacuum-braked wagonload freight network had more or less disappeared, to be replaced by the air-braked Speedlink network. On 25 June 1983, No. 37248 heads west through Pembrey and Bury Port with a Speedlink freight trip working. The two former BR ferry vans will be acting as barrier wagons probably for a wagon of government stores for one of the MOD depots in West Wales.

The Cardiff Canton-allocated Class 101 DMUs were usually outbased at Swansea to work services over the Central Wales line and to West Wales. Class 101 Metro-Cammell set C801 (formed of vehicles Nos 51446 and 51517) calls at Pembrey and Burry Port on a service from Swansea on 15 June 1983. This was one of six sets at the time that operated as a 'power twin' set for use on the Central Wales line, with the centre trailer car having been removed.

The 10.17 Swansea to Fishguard Harbour stands at Carmarthen on 6 June 1983, having arrived behind No. 47536. Carmarthen station is effectively a terminus; trains must reverse here and No. 47536 has been detached. Meanwhile, No. 47575 has been attached to the rear to work the train forward.

When Class 33s took over passenger services in West Wales, they remained allocated to Eastleigh. The locos worked a three-day diagram, which allowed them to return to Eastleigh for maintenance. On 6 June 1983, No. 33021 departs from Whitland with the 14.50 Swansea to Milford Haven service.

Swindon-built cross-country Class 120 DMUs had been regular performers in West Wales and over the Central Wales route, but by 1983 only two sets remained. Set C616 (formed of vehicles Nos 51782, 59681 and 51790) approaches Haverfordwest with the 13.23 Milford Haven to Swansea service on 6 June 1983. The unit is fitted with headlights for working over the Central Wales route.

There were a number of collieries in West Wales forwarding coal by rail, with locos and train crews being based at Pantyffynnon. On 4 November 1983, one of the Landore-allocated Class 08s, No. 08662, is seen shunting at Betws Drift Mine near Ammanford. The drift mine had only started producing anthracite coal in 1978. The loaded MDOs will now make the short journey via Pantyffynnon station to Wernos Washery.